Fake News:
do YOU know what to bel...

Written by Paul Harrison
Illustrated by Mike Phillips

Contents

Collins

1 Introduction

What is fake news? The simple definition is that a fake news story is a story that isn't true. However, fake news is a bit more complex than that. There are different types of fake news and these stories are spread for different reasons.

Fake news can be as innocent as a joke or a bit of fun, but many types of fake news are seriously bad news. A newspaper can choose the facts it includes in a story to make its readers react in a certain way. A business can use fake news to harm a competitor or to boost their own sales. A criminal may use fake news to try and steal information or money from an unsuspecting victim. Fake news can even be used to try and bring down a government or influence an election result.

On the rise

The term "fake news" really came to the public's attention back in 2016. The politician Donald Trump, who was trying to get elected as president of the USA, often used the term to **discredit** stories he didn't believe. It was also used against him. In that year alone, the use of "fake news" as a saying increased by 365%. It became such a famous term that the *Collins Dictionary* made it their word of the year for 2017.

collinsWOTY

2 Early fakes

There is nothing new about fake news, though. In ancient Greece, the **philosopher** and **botanist** Theophrastus described 30 different types of person in his work *Characters*. One of these people was the "Newshound" who enjoys spreading false stories.

Royal rebellion

During the reign of the British King George II (born 1683 – died 1760), people spread false news about his health as a way of trying to stir up a revolution to overthrow him from the throne. The rumours spread quickly, thanks to the printing press which allowed people to print the rumours and display them.

Don't believe everything in the paper

Newspapers have been known to tell fake stories on purpose. One **notorious** case was printed by the *New York Sun* in 1835. It claimed that astronomers had seen evidence of life on the moon. The article went into detail about the types of weird and wonderful creatures they had discovered. The following month, the newspaper admitted it had made up the stories, but by this point the number of people reading the paper had greatly increased and helped the paper's profits.

Fake news is designed to affect how a person feels about a topic. This has been used on a global scale, too – even during wars.

some of the moon creatures described in the article

3 World at war

Telling lies and **smearing** opponents can be used by politicians at home, but fake news has also been used as a weapon of war against other nations. Warfare is expensive and costs lives – fake news, on the other hand, can weaken an enemy country without having to fire a bullet. Fake news is a type of **propaganda**, and propaganda has been used as a weapon of war for centuries. A government may choose to exaggerate, lie or present only positive information to boost the morale of its own people. In contrast, it may present negative information or false stories to weaken enemy morale. The key with propaganda is to get the message to people before the enemy government can stop it.

During the Second World War, Germany used to broadcast radio programmes to Britain which would say how strong Germany was and how weak Britain was by comparison. They would also drop leaflets over the UK with the same message. In return, Britain and America used planes to drop thousands of propaganda leaflets over an enemy city or area. With so many leaflets being dropped, it was almost guaranteed that people would see them.

The Battle of the Atlantic is being lost!

The reasons why:

1. German U-boats, German bombers and the German fleet sink and seriously damage between them every month, a total of 700 000 to 1 million tons of British and allied shipping.

2. All attempts at finding a satisfactory means of defence against the German U-boats or the German bombers have failed disastrously.

3. Even President Roosevelt has openly stated that for every five ships sunk by Germany, Britain and America between them can only build two new ones. All attempts to launch a larger shipbuilding programme in America have failed.

4. Britain is no longer in a position to secure her avenues of supply. The population of Britain has to do with about half the ration that the population of Germany gets. Britain, herself, can only support 40% of her population from her own resources in spite of the attempts made to increase the amount of land under cultivation. If the war is continued until 1942, 60% of the population of Britain will starve!

All this means that starvation in Britain is not to be staved off. At the most it can be postponed, but whether starvation comes this year or at the beginning of next doesn't make a ha'porth of difference. Britain must starve because she is being cut off from her supplies.

Britain's losing the Battle of the Atlantic means

Britain's losing the war!

This German propaganda leaflet was dropped over the east of England in 1941. It told people they would starve because war in the Atlantic Ocean was cutting off food supplies.

This kind of propaganda works very well if people in the enemy country already think that things are not going well, as they are more likely to believe the messages. However, if the enemy is feeling confident then people are more likely to ignore the propaganda.

4 Making money

Spotting fake news is important when money is involved, as the idea of getting rich can make people do odd and – in some cases – highly illegal things. When big business is involved this can mean **big bucks**, but fake news can involve even the smallest businesses too.

Lying for profit

You can make money from fake news, as American university **graduate** Cameron Harris realised when he was looking for a way to pay off the money he had borrowed as a student. In 2016, he bought the internet domain name ChristianTimesNewspaper.com and charged money for companies to advertise on the site. This is how many websites make money. The more people that visit a website, the more money the website can make from advertisers. One day, Harris posted a fake news story on his site and noticed that more people read this fake news than the real news stories he had posted. Soon he was posting more fake news and earning more and more money. But why did more people read the fake stories?

Harris believed that people wanted to find evidence to support their own point of view. So, for example, if someone wants to believe a certain politician is up to no good and Harris posted a story saying just that, the story would get read and shared around.

The value of the website climbed and climbed – until new rules on the internet forced sites like Harris's to change how they operated. It seems you can make money from fake news, but not forever.

Macedonian mischief

It's not just individuals who make money from fake news –
sometimes companies are set up to do just that. When lots
of fake news stories started appearing on American **social
media platforms** during the 2016 USA presidential elections,
it turned out that many of them came from an unlikely
source – a small city called Veles in the European country
of North Macedonia. Just as Cameron Harris discovered,
people would read any article that supported their own point
of view. Also, as with Harris's website, advertisers would pay
a lot of money to have their advertisements appear next to
these popular stories. Because people in America use social
media a lot, companies in Macedonia targeted readers in
the USA in order to make money.

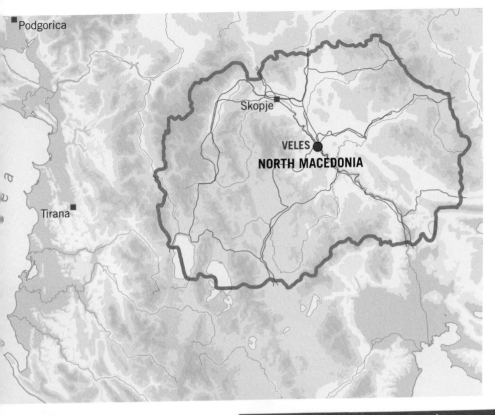

Podgorica

Skopje

VELES
NORTH MACEDONIA

Tirana

TRUMP R

48.9%

2,676,543

New Yorkers follow the election results in Times Square

STEP INSIDE. SNAP YOUR PHOTO. GET UP HERE.

VORNADO

11

Gone phishing

Making money by spreading fake news isn't always illegal – unless the people involved are trying to get their hands on something that doesn't belong to them. The practice known as **phishing** is designed to do just that. Fishing is trying to catch fish; phishing is trying to catch valuable personal information from people. Using emails to go phishing is one of the most common ways criminals try to get cash from unsuspecting victims.

Often a phishing email will ask the victim for help.
For example, the criminal may pretend they are someone
else and that they have a lot of money which they need to
move to a bank account in the victim's country. Or they
may even ask for help and money for an emergency airfare.
The criminal sometimes promises that they will pay
the victim some money if they are able to help. All they
need is the victim's bank account details.

Phishing attempts can look very convincing. Criminals can copy the logos of real companies and even government departments, in an attempt to make their fake emails look like the real thing. For example, people in the UK have received emails claiming to be from HMRC (which stands for Her Majesty's Revenue and Customs, a government department that deals with tax) claiming that the person either owes money or is due money back. Attached to the email is a form the victim needs to fill in which, in reality, installs **malware** on the victim's computer. People are likely to fall for this kind of scam, either because of the promise of getting money or to avoid getting into trouble.

Top Tip!

To keep yourself safe from phishing attempts, NEVER click on any links in these dodgy emails. Instead, go to the real website which the email claims to be from and find out if the email is genuine or not. Remember, banks and other organisations will never ask you for personal information via email, so never share your own details with the sender of an email.

As soon as the criminal has the victim's bank or credit card details, they can make payments using the victim's money. Their methods are very simple and lots of people fall for this kind of thing every year.

TO: B. Smart
From: Hoo Nose

You have won our kompetition! Your the lucky person who has won first prize! Click **hear** to claim it!

Would you fall for this?

5 Bad medicine

Not all fake news is a deliberate lie or a con trick to steal money off unsuspecting people. Sometimes, fake news takes the form of bad advice. People believe something is true and end up spreading their idea – and when they are offering medical advice, the results can be awful.

No good for vampires or pandemics

In 2020, the world was gripped by a new illness called COVID-19. It stood out for a number of reasons: it spread across the globe very quickly; very little was known about it; and there was no vaccine to prevent it. When science couldn't provide immediate answers, people looked elsewhere for solutions.

This is exactly the kind of situation where fake news flourishes.

Before vaccines and treatments had been developed, there were all sorts of claims about what would cure or prevent coronavirus. One such claim was that eating garlic would stop you from catching it. Garlic as part of a balanced diet will keep you healthy, but it won't stop you from catching coronavirus. One woman reportedly ate so much garlic it made her throat swell and she ended up going to hospital to have her throat treated!

Deadly advice

Occasionally, fake news spreads because the story comes from a reliable source. In 1998, a study appeared in a medical journal called *The Lancet*. The study suggested that a series of injections (or vaccinations, as they are called) given to babies to protect them from serious illnesses could cause autism. Autism is a condition that affects the way a person thinks, reacts to situations and communicates with other people.

It was worrying news but also incorrect. The study was flawed and the doctor who carried out the study got into a lot of trouble. Unfortunately, the news of the study's results had already been shared and some people refused to have their babies vaccinated. This led to outbreaks of serious infections, such as measles, which hadn't happened for a number of years previously.

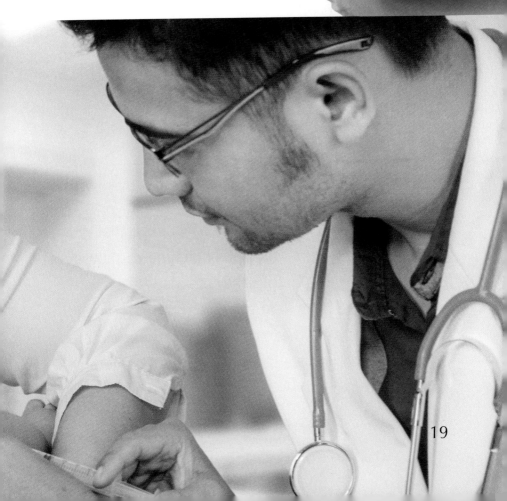

6 Myths, monsters and things that go bump in the night

Fake news works because people will believe all sorts of things, whether there is any real evidence for them or not. Take, for example, mythical monsters, alien spaceships or ghosts.

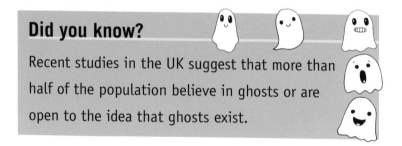

Did you know?

Recent studies in the UK suggest that more than half of the population believe in ghosts or are open to the idea that ghosts exist.

Fake photos

People have always wanted to see evidence that ghosts exist, which is why photographs claiming to show ghosts are popular. Unfortunately, they are also fake news. Scientists have been able to prove that these images are either mistakes that happened when the pictures were produced or have been the result of camera or computer trickery.

In the early days of photography, people such as William H Mumler made a career of being a "ghost-photographer". He had worked out how to make other ghostly figures appear in his pictures by printing two images onto the same photograph. He managed to fool experts and the public for many years – making a good living from it in the process. He was later taken to court in 1869 accused of being a fraud. Although Mumler was **acquitted** – because there was not enough proof at the time – the suspicion that it was all a **hoax** ruined his business.

Is there anybody out there?

The universe is so big and stretches so far, it feels remarkable that Earth is the only planet with life on it. Are there other worlds out there with alien life on them – or is this idea fake news too? There's been no scientific proof so far, but that hasn't stopped people from trying to fool us into thinking there has.

Is it a bird? Is it a plane?

In the 1950s, tales began to surface of people spotting strange flying objects that didn't look like any known aircraft. These were called Unidentified Flying Objects, or UFOs for short. They were also called flying saucers, because the UFOs were often shaped like discs. As it turned out, these photographs were easy to fake. Any circular object, such as car parts, or bowls, could be flung into the air and photographed – and the blurry shots looked like strange aircraft.

Not all these photographs were done as deliberate tricks to fool people. Other pictures of UFOs turned out to be naturally occurring events, such as weirdly-shaped clouds, spherical lightning known as ball lightning, or **meteors**.

photos taken in Michigan, USA in 1947 and Melbourne, Australia in 1966

23

Model hoax

For UFO hunters, one of the most famous places to try and visit is Roswell in the USA. It was claimed that a flying saucer crashed there, and that the army took all the evidence away and stored it in a top-secret base nearby. Although the evidence suggests that the aircraft in the crash was actually just a type of balloon used to help predict the weather, that hasn't stopped the stories. There were even claims that bodies of the aliens, or Martians, had been taken from the site, too.

Then, in 1995, a video emerged, supposedly showing doctors examining the body of what was claimed to be one of the Roswell Martians. The so-called "alien autopsy" video caused a sensation – but was it genuine? The answer was no – it was an elaborate hoax. In 2017, a filmmaker called Spyros Melaris admitted that he and another man called Ray Santilli had made the whole thing up. The film was a fake and had been made in London, not in a secret US Army base. The alien was a model, not a Martian, and the doctors were just actors.

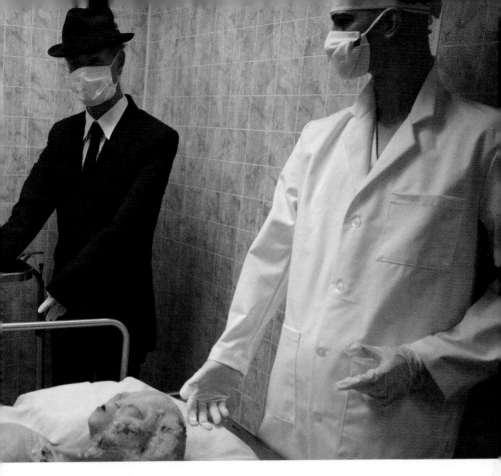

Myths and monsters

Are there really monsters lurking in the quiet corners
of our world, or are these reported sightings more fake
than fact? There are still many things we don't know about
our planet. The bottom of the seas and lakes remains
largely unexplored. Thick forests are yet to show us
their secrets. Is it possible that strange animals are yet
to be discovered?

Not Nessie

Loch Ness is a long, deep lake (or loch, as it's known locally) in Scotland. It has long been rumoured to be the home of a mysterious creature described as being either a huge serpent or a prehistoric monster. The creature has been named Nessie, and thousands of people have gone to the loch in search of it. In 1934, a **grainy** photograph, supposedly taken by a doctor called Robert Kenneth Wilson, was published in the *Daily Mail* newspaper. It seemed to show a creature with a long neck swimming across the loch. This was just the evidence that Nessie Hunters were looking for! Except it wasn't – it was actually a toy submarine with a fake serpent's head on. It was the work of a couple of hoaxers called Christopher Spurling and Marmaduke Wetherell.

26

Amazing apes?

All across the world, there are tales of ape-like creatures that walk on two legs. There are stories about the Yeti from the mountains of the Himalaya, the Orang Pendek from Sumatra in Indonesia and the North American Sasquatch (or Bigfoot, as it's also known). Is there any evidence that such creatures exist?

In 1967, Roger Patterson and Bob Gimlin released a film they had made in the forests of Northern California. It seemed to show a large ape-like creature striding towards the trees. The film became famous and was seen all around the world. Was this the legendary Bigfoot? The filmmakers always claimed that the footage was real, but lots of people said it had to be a fake. Then in 2004, one of their friends, called Bob Hieronimus, said that the footage actually showed him wearing an ape suit. He claimed he would have stayed quiet about it if he had been paid the 1,000 dollars he had been promised for wearing it.

27

7 A day of pranks and jokes

The origins of April Fools' Day are unclear, but what is certain is you have to be on your guard so you don't get fooled by a bit of good-natured fake news yourself!

Modern mayhem

One of the earliest April Fools' Day pranks recorded happened in 1698, when people were persuaded that they could see lions being washed at the Tower of London. Apparently, lots of people fell for the joke and this kind of prank remains popular today.

Show us the lions

28

PLANET OF THE APPS

Gorillas get iPads as aid to alertness

EXCLUSIVE by BRIAN FLYNN

A GORILLA prods the new toy which scientists hope will transform the way primates are kept alert and happy in zoos — an iPad.

Animal behaviour experts handed out the gadgets to five apes in an experiment.

The super-smart gorillas quickly learned to turn the screens on and off and seem fascinated by the colours and pictures.

Amazingly not a **SINGLE** one of the five tablets which download apps has been broken since being given out at Port Lympne wild animal park three weeks ago.

Head keeper Phil Ridges said yesterday: "We thought they would bang them on rocks but they carry them round as if they were babies."

Boffins at the University of Kent, Canterbury, are behind the trial, which is being monitored by Apple.

Phil said: "Keeping gorillas stimulated has been a challenge — but they are fascinated by these things."

The park in Hythe, Kent, cares for more than 20 endangered western lowland gorillas. Readers can adopt one for £3 a month at aspinallfoundation.org.   b.flynn@the-sun.co.uk

WELCOME TO PORT LYMPNE

In 2011, The Sun *newspaper ran this April Fools story. However, staff at a zoo in the United States were inspired by the hoax story to start weekly tablet sessions with their orangutans, which became very popular!*

The technology company Google enjoys an April Fools' Day joke. One year, it claimed that its search engine could read your thoughts! All you had to do was stare at the screen while thinking about what you wanted to look for.

Of course, this was nonsense, but Google played a second prank by flashing up error messages on the screen with suggested reasons why it hadn't worked. One said it would only work if you clapped three times and said, "I believe".

Tasty trees

One of the most famous April Fools' Day hoaxes of
all time was shown on British television in 1957.
The BBC reported on a bumper harvest of spaghetti in
Switzerland. The programme showed women picking
strands of spaghetti from trees and bushes and laying it on
the ground to dry. As you may know, spaghetti is a pasta
made from durum wheat and water – it certainly does not
grow on trees. However, lots of people fell for the joke.

The hoax was so convincing that people rang the BBC to find out where they could buy one of the bushes. One of the reasons for its success was that people trusted the source the information was coming from. In addition, the presenter of the programme was a highly-respected journalist, Richard Dimbleby, so the story had the feeling of being **authentic**. The hoax also contained enough information to make the story believable. Finally, spaghetti was not as popular in Britain then as it is now, so a lot of people were ignorant about how it was made.

Where can I get my hands on one of these spaghetti trees?

8 Mistakes and urban legends

Sometimes, fake news can be spread with the best intentions. An honest mistake can lead to a rumour which then gets spread and lots of people end up believing it.

The Queen is dead!

When members of the British Royal Navy got a message in early December 2019 asking them to return to their base at Royal Navy Air Station Yeovilton, they knew something was up. When they saw it was for "Operation London Bridge" they knew it was serious – because that was the **codename** for what happened when Queen Elizabeth II died. It was actually just a drill – a practice to make sure everyone knew what they had to do when the Queen did actually die, but not everyone realised that. Unfortunately, word got out that Operation London Bridge was happening, and people thought the Queen really was dead. The rumour travelled quickly and the only way it could be stopped was for the Royal Family to tell everyone the Queen was alive and well!

33

Modern legends

Urban legends are fake
stories that refuse to
die no matter how many
times people point out
that they aren't true.
Some of these tales are
decades old, like the story
of the circus performer who
was swallowed by a hippo,
and some are a bit newer.

Modern technology can help to prove some urban legends
are not true. Take the idea that we only use 10% of our
brains when thinking – just think what kind of genius
you could be if you could use the other 90%! No one is
sure where this idea came
from, but unfortunately it's
not true. Machines called
MRI scanners measure
the brain's activity and it
turns out that we use all of
our brain power already –
which is a shame!

Modern mythmaking

In the past, the way people could access news was quite limited. There were newspapers, radio and television programmes. There were no 24-hour news channels and, more importantly, no internet or social media. Now, people can get news whenever they like, from whomever they like. This means people's access to fake news is greater than ever before. No matter where you are in the world, if you have access to the internet, you can be exposed to fake news stories every minute of the day.

No filter

While social media can be an excellent tool for getting news and information out quickly, its speed and availability can be a problem. A fake story or rumour can spread right around the world in no time at all. The main issue with social media and some internet-based news sites is that in many cases there's no way of knowing whether you should believe them or not. With television, radio or newspapers, stories are meant to go through some sort of fact-checking process and you know exactly who is telling you the story. With the internet, literally anyone can set up a **social media profile** and post stories. Not knowing who these people are or what they stand for makes the news they are sharing unreliable – whether they are spreading untrue rumours about celebrities or predicting the end of the world.

Bad robots

Sometimes stories are not even posted by a person. Bots are computer programs that can work independently, posting information on social media sites. They can be used for things like updating football scores on a website. They can also be used to post fake news. One recent study showed that nearly half of the posts about coronavirus on one social media platform had been made by bots. The reasons why someone would program bots to spread fake news might vary, but it's always the case that you should be wary about what you read.

Bots aren't really robots. They are computer programs written by humans.

Holidaying from home

Just how easy is it to create a fake story? Dutch student Zilla van den Born proved how a little time and effort could convince even her closest friends and family that she was doing something she wasn't. In 2014, Zilla went for a five-week-long holiday to Thailand – at least, that's what everyone thought. Over the course of her holiday, Zilla posted photographs from her trip on her social media platforms, showing she was having a wonderful time in Asia. Except she wasn't – she was still in Amsterdam and was faking all the photographs!

Using props she found at home or in the shops, she managed to carefully stage a series of photographs to make it look like she was in a different country. It was very clever, but she had done it to prove that we shouldn't believe everything we see on the internet. Zilla was particularly concerned about the effects of looking at social media too much. She wanted to show that people shouldn't judge themselves by comparing their own lives to what other people post online. Your own life might seem **drab** by comparison, but what you are comparing yourself to might not be real in the first place!

Zilla photoshopped herself into different locations

Back from the dead

Deepfakes are films or recordings that recreate what a person looks or sounds like but aren't real. This special effect uses powerful computers to map a person's face and superimpose it on top of an actor's face. What the program does is to recreate how a person moves their face and the way they speak. Using deepfakes can be a way of seeing long-dead film stars in new films, or, more worryingly, a way to spread fake news.

People can make deepfakes of politicians or celebrities and get them to say whatever they like. This can cause embarrassment for the person being faked. In extreme cases, it could cause international problems. Can you imagine the leader of one country saying they would invade another one? It's all possible with a deepfake film.

the British Queen in a deepfaked video made by Channel 4 in the UK to draw attention to the dangers of deepfaking

9 Stories that live forever

There's a famous quotation that says, "If you tell a lie often enough it becomes the truth". It means that if you hear or see something enough times it becomes believable. Part of the problem with stories on the internet is that they never really go away. If just one person has a copy of a picture or a piece of fake news, then it can be circulated all over again. A story can travel from one person's room all around the world in a matter of minutes.

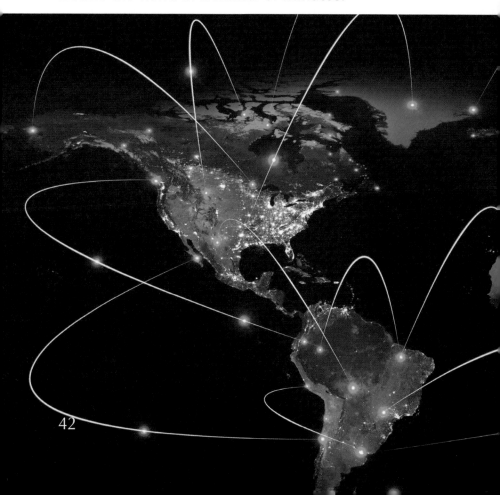

Faking it

People are more likely to believe something if they already suspect it to be true. They are more likely to share stories or points of view they agree with, whether or not these stories are actually fake. That is part of the problem with believing everything a stranger tells you – and they may not even be a real person to begin with.

10 Fighting against the fakes

There has never been as much fake news around as there is today. From incorrect stories, to rumours, to propaganda, to honest mistakes, fake news is everywhere. So how can you be sure whether what you are reading, watching or hearing is real or not? How do you know you are not being tricked into doing something? Fortunately, there are certain things that you can look out for to help you fight the fakes.

No names, no news

If you read a story on the internet and there are no names mentioned – either in the article or saying who wrote it, then be wary. If you don't know who has written it, how do you know you can trust it? You probably wouldn't believe something a stranger told you as much as a story from someone you know. Use the same principle when looking online.

Popular doesn't mean right

Just because a story has been shared lots of times or has lots of likes, it doesn't mean that the story is true. We've seen how fake news can be spread by accident or on purpose. When a famous person posts a story then it usually gets shared or liked a great deal. Famous people are just as likely to be **duped** by fake news as anybody else so they might be spreading unreliable information themselves.

Be afraid

Fake news spreads quickly when it plays on people's emotions – especially fear or worry. People are likely to share stories that warn them of some kind of danger. This is why fake stories about health scares or conspiracy theories about companies and governments doing illegal things spread so quickly. Be wary of stories whose message is "be afraid" – especially if there's little real evidence to back up the story.

During the COVID-19 pandemic, fake news stories told people that 5G phone masts and networks were helping to spread the virus. This wasn't true.

Double-check

Don't believe everything you read. It's always a good idea to check if something is right by seeing if you can find the same information anywhere else. If you can find it somewhere else – especially if it's from a source you can trust – then it might well be true. Be careful though. If the story sounds exactly the same on the second source, then it's likely someone has just copied it from somewhere else.

There are usually ways of spotting fake news, but you have to be paying attention. Fake news spreads when people aren't careful about what they read and what they share. Be alert and don't be a victim of fake news.

Is this a real news story?

Check the address

Criminals and fakers will often pretend to be someone they aren't. Emails might claim to come from someone you trust but are actually clever fakes. Always check to see that the email address looks like an official address.

Also check the spelling – criminals often write company names that look like the real one at first glance but might have one letter different from the original.

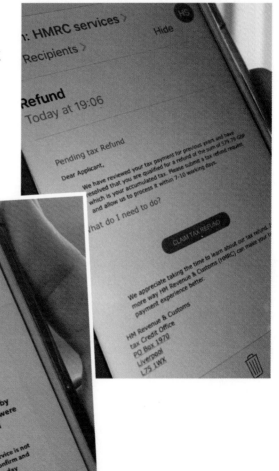

Can you spot a fake?

What should you look for when you see pictures like this?
Is this really the Loch Ness monster?

Have scientists really invented a cube-shaped apple?

Answers:

☐ Is the object as big as people are claiming – is there anything in the picture to compare the size of the object to?

☐ Why is the image so blurry – is it to hide what the image really is?

☐ The edges of objects or people are difficult to fake. Do the edges look convincing?

☐ Do the colours and lighting look the same across the photograph?

Glossary

acquitted freed from a criminal charge

authentic genuine / true

big bucks lots of money

botanist a scientist who studies plants

codename a word used for secrecy instead of a real name

cyber criminals criminals who operate online

deepfakes films or recordings of someone that isn't real

discredit to say something is bad or untrustworthy

drab dull/not colourful

duped fooled or deceived by something

graduate someone who has successfully completed a course of study

grainy not smooth or clear, rough, like it's full of spots / grains

hoax a trick

malware programs that deliberately harm computers, sometimes in order to get information or to demand money from the victim

meteors pieces of rock or metal that fall to Earth from outer space

notorious famous for being bad or terrible

philosopher someone who studies the nature of life, thought and knowledge

phishing sending an email pretending to be from a trustworthy company or person for the purpose of fraud

propaganda information used to discredit enemies or to highlight a government's point of view

smearing discrediting public figures by using lies

social media platforms mobile or internet services which allow the user to connect with other users

social media profile description of a person owning a social media account

source the origin of a story

FAKE or REAL?

UNICORNS FOUND ON THE MOON

ORANGUTANS USE TABLETS TO COMMUNICATE

55

Ideas for reading

Written by Gill Matthews
Primary Literacy Consultant

Reading objectives:

- summarise the main ideas drawn from more than one paragraph, identifying key details that support the main ideas
- retrieve, record and present information from non-fiction
- participate in discussions about books that are read to them and those they can read for themselves, building on their own and others' ideas and challenging view courteously
- explain and discuss their understanding of what they have read, including through formal presentations and debates, maintaining a focus on the topic and using notes where necessary

Spoken language objectives:

- give well-structured descriptions, explanations and narratives for different purposes, including for expressing feelings
- participate in discussions, presentations, performances, role play/ improvisations and debates

Curriculum links: Relationships education – Online relationships; Health education – Internet safety and harms

Interest words: seriously, failed, disastrously, only, starvation, starve

Resources: ICT

Build a context for reading

- Explore the covers. Check children's understanding of the title. What do they think it means?
- Ask what kind of book children think this is and what they expect to find in it. Discuss the kind of features that usually appear in non-fiction books.
- Turn to the contents page. Ask children where they think they will find an overview of the book.
- Read the introduction on pp2–3 aloud. Explore children's understanding of fake news and why people and organisations spread it.

Understand and apply reading strategies

- Return to the contents page. Explain that you thought fake news was a very recent thing. Ask children which section they think might tell us something different.